# Made for praise

**VOLUME 4**

## FOR YOUNGER CHILDREN

**Dovetail Music**

A division of Genevox

ISBN 0-7673-3522-8

© Copyright 1998 GENEVOX (a div. of GMG), Nashville, TN 37234.

All Scripture quotations are from the Holy Bible, New International Version
© 1973, 1978, 1984 International Bible Society, unless otherwise noted.

## *Made for Praise*® *Volume 4*
## *Younger Children*
## CREDITS
---

Music Arranger and Producer - Dick Tunney

Music Typsetting - Allen Tuten, Compute-A-Chart

Video - Southern Video, Inc.

Art Supervisor - Jimmy Bass, Hillview Lake Publishing Co., Inc.

Layout - Chris Whitmer, Hillview Lake Publishing Co., Inc.

Illustrations - Ron Wheeler

Teaching and Worship Plans - Written by Pamela Clampitt Vandewalker
with Cherry G. Tippins and David W. Vandewalker

Literary Layout and Design Editor - David W. Vandewalker

Editor-in-Chief and Design Coordinator - Cherry G. Tippins

# CONTENTS

## SONGS*

| | |
|---|---|
| A Mother's Love | 5 |
| Beautiful Lamb | 7 |
| Change My Heart, O God | 9 |
| Do This | 11 |
| Fairest Lord Jesus | 13 |
| Hold Me | 15 |
| Jesus Born On This Day | 17 |
| Jesus Is The Banner | 19 |
| Made For Praise | 21 |
| Softly And Tenderly | 24 |
| More Than Anything | 39 |
| Nobody But Noah | 41 |
| Psalm 91 Lullaby | 43 |
| Seek First The Kingdom | 45 |
| Sunday School Medley | 47 |
| Tell Him Thank You | 52 |
| There Is Power In The Wonderful Name | 53 |
| Whale Of A Tale | 55 |
| With My Whole Heart | 57 |
| You Are Always In His Sight | 59 |

## COLOR TEACHING PAGES

| | |
|---|---|
| Choral Reading - Fairest Lord Jesus | 25 |
| Pictorial Account Of Noah | 26 |
| Whale Of A Tale - Fish "Pulse" Activity | 28 |
| Dynamic Scripture - Seek First The Kingdom | 29 |
| Musical Computer Tool Box | 30 |
| Your Awesome Singing Machine | 31 |
| Jonah - Whale Of A Tale Drama | 32 |
| Fire Drill | 34 |
| Investigative Report - News About Noah | 36 |
| Add-A-Word | 38 |

*All piano accompaniments are in *Made For Praise*® for Younger Children, Volume 4 Leader's Guide (ISBN 0-7673-3463-9).

# A Mother's Love

Words and Music by
DICK and MELODIE TUNNEY
Arranged by Dick Tunney

With feeling (♩ = 80)

SOLO (Child)

Thank You, Lord, for a moth-er's love, Love that was born with a Child. Her eyes can see with wis-dom; there's hope be-hind her smile. God has cre-at-ed a moth-er's heart with strength to guide our way And teach us of our God a-bove. Thank You, Lord, for a moth-er's love.

SOLO (Adult Female)

E-ven as Je-sus walked the earth He was placed in a moth-er's care. To hold Him close to calm His fears, His deep-est thoughts to share. And as Ma-ry's heart knew the

For accompaniment see Leader's Guide, p.27

© Copyright 1997 Sony/ATV Tunes LLC/Molto Bravo! Music, Inc./Dick and Mel Music (ASCAP). All rights administered by Sony/ATV Music Publishing, 8 Music Sq. W., Nashville, TN 37203. Used by Permission.

greatest joy, And felt the deepest pain.
God gave His strength from above, Thank You, Lord, for a mother's love.

**CHOIR**

Thank You, Lord, for a mother's love, Her children call her blessed. Grace and glory will be the crown of a heart that You possess. The greatest gift of a mother's love is found upon her knees. Trusting in our God above, Thank You, Lord, for a mother's love. Thank You, Lord, for a mother's love.

# Beautiful Lamb

Words and Music by
STEPHEN BARR
Arranged by Dick Tunney

Gently (♩ = 116)   CHOIR

1. Beau - ti - ful, beau - ti - ful Lamb, Sav - ior of all that I am. Right - teous and ho - ly, No oth - er is wor - thy. For the One who was slain, I will stand. Beau - ti - ful, beau - ti - ful Lamb.

2. Won - der - ful, won - der - ful King, Mas - ter of all liv - ing things. I bow be - fore You, To love and a - dore You. To en - throne You on prais - es I sing. Won - der - ful, won - der - ful King.

Glo - ri - ous, glo - ri - ous Lord, Wor - shiped, hon - ored, a - dored. Vic - to - rious o'er the cross,

*For accompaniment see Leader's Guide, p.37*

© Copyright 1998 Sony/ATV Tunes LLC/Molto Bravo! Music, Inc./Dick & Mel Music (ASCAP). All rights administered by Sony/ATV Music Publishing, 8 Music Sq. W., Nashville, TN 37203. Used by permission.

8

Je - sus the Son of God. He who will reign ev - er - more. Glo - ri - ous, glo - ri - ous

*rit.* *f a tempo*

Lord! Beau - ti - ful, beau - ti - ful Lamb, Sav - ior of all that I am. Righ - teous and ho - ly, No oth - er is wor - thy. For the One who was slain, I will stand. Beau - ti - ful, beau - ti - ful Lamb. Beau - ti - ful, beau - ti - ful

*rit.*

Lamb. Beau - ti - ful, beau - ti - ful

*mf a tempo* *rit.*

Lamb.

# Change My Heart, O God

Words and Music by
EDDIE ESPINOSA
Arranged by Dick Tunney

Gently (♩ = 102)

CHOIR *mp*

Change my heart, O God, Make it ev-er true.

Change my heart, O God, May I be like You.

Change my heart, O God, Make it ev-er true. Change my heart, O God, May I be like You.

*First time - SOLO*
*Second time - CHOIR*

You are the Pot - ter, I am the

*For accompaniment see Leader's Guide, p.49*

© Copyright 1982 by Mercy/Vineyard Publishing (admin. by Music Services, Inc.)
All Rights Reserved. Used by Permission.

clay. Mold me and make me,

*Second time to Coda* 𝄌    D.S. al Coda

This is what I pray.

𝄌 CODA

pray. Change my heart, O

God, Make it ev - er

true. Change my heart, O God,

May I be like You. Change my heart, O

God, May I be like You.

*rit.*

# Do This!

Words and Music by
RUTH ELAINE SCHRAM
Arranged by Dick Tunney

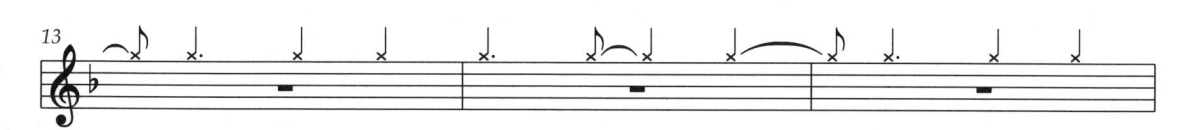

Gently (♩ = 120)

CHOIR *mf*

I am fear-ful-ly and won-der-ful-ly made; When I think of how You made me, I'm a-mazed. I can *stand up, sit down, and put my hands up and I can sing a song of praise and then do this:

Clap:

*In rhythm with the words, stand, sit back down, and raise both hands.

For accompaniment see Leader's Guide, p.57

© Copyright 1998 Van Ness Press, Inc. (ASCAP).
Distributed by GENEVOX (a div. of GMG), Nashville, TN 37234.

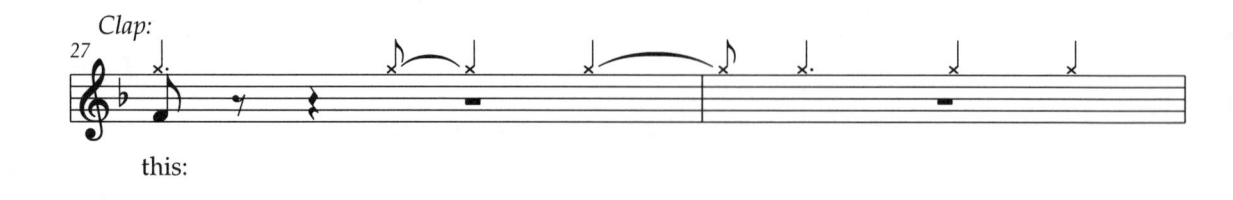

I am fear-ful-ly and won-der-ful-ly made. When I think of how You made me I'm a-mazed. I can stand up, sit down, and put my hands up, and I can sing a song of praise and then do

*Clap:*

this:

And I can sing a song of praise and then do this

# Fairest Lord Jesus

Words Anonymous German Hymn

Music from *Schlesische Volkslieder*
Arranged by Dick Tunney

Brightly (♩ = 96) CHOIR

Fair - est Lord Je - sus, Rul - er of all na - ture, O Thou of God and man the Son; Thee will I cher - ish, Thee will I hon - or, Thou, my soul's glo - ry, joy, and crown.

Fair is the sun - shine, Fair - er still the moon - light And all the twin - kling, star - ry host; Je - sus shines bright - er, Je - sus shines pur - er Than all the an - gels heav'n can

*For accompaniment see Leader's Guide, p.67*

© Copyright 1998 Sony/ATV Tunes LLC/Molto Bravo! Music, Inc./Dick & Mel Music (ASCAP). All rights administered by Sony/ATV Music Publishing, 8 Music Sq. W., Nashville, TN 37203. Used by permission.

boast. Beau - ti - ful

Sav - ior, Lord of all na - tions, Son of

God and Son of man! Glo - ry and

hon - or, Praise, ad - o - ra - tion, Now and for - ev - er -

**PART 1**

more be Thine! Now

**PART 2** *(opt.)*

more be, Fair - est Lord Je -

and for - ev - er - more be

sus, more be

*rit.*

Thine!

*rit.*

Thine!

# Hold Me

Words and Music by
STEVEN BARR
Arranged by Dick Tunney

Gently (♩ = 104)

Hold me, hold me, Je-sus hold me close. Love me, tell me how You'll nev-er let me go.

*Third time to Coda*

When my heart is sad and lone-ly, Or feel-ing just a lit-tle a-fraid. I re-mem-ber how much You love me, and that You'll hold me when I

*For accompaniment see Leader's Guide, p.79*

© Copyright 1998 Sony/ATV Tunes LLC/Molto Bravo! Music, Inc./Dick & Mel Music (ASCAP). All rights administered by Sony/ATV Music Publishing, 8 Music Sq. W., Nashville, TN 37203. Used by permission.

pray. go. SOLO If I'm fright-ened while I'm dream-ing, Or I'm scared to go to sleep. I'll re-mem-ber You're be-side me; So my dreams will all be sweet.

*D.S. al Coda*

CODA

go. Hold me, hold me, Je-sus, hold me close. Love me, tell me how You'll nev-er let me go, how You'll nev-er let me go.

# Jesus Born on this Day

Words and Music by
MARIAH CAREY and WALTER AFANASIEFF
Arranged by Dick Tunney

*Simply* (♩ = 92)

1. To- day a
2. Be- hold the

Child is born on earth, To- day a Child is born on
Lamb of God has come, Be- hold the Lamb of God has

earth. To- day the glo- ry of God shines ev-'ry-where for
come. Be- hold the Sav- ior is born, sing of His love to

all the world. Oh, Je- sus,
ev- 'ry- one. Oh, Je- sus,

born on this day. He is our Light and sal- va-
born on this day. Heav- en- ly Child in a man-

tion. Oh, Je- sus,
ger. Oh, Je- sus,

born on this day, He is the King of all na-
born on this day, He is our Lord and our Sav-

tions.
ior.

*For accompaniment see Leader's Guide, p.89*

© Copyright 1994 Sony/ATV Songs, Inc./Rye Songs (BMI)/Sony/ATV Tunes LLC/Wallyworld Music (ASCAP). All rights administered by Sony/ATV Music Publishing, 8 Music Sq. W., Nashvile, TN 37203. Used by Permission.

18

# Jesus Is the Banner

Words and Music by
JOHN CHISUM and NANCY GORDON
Arranged by Dick Tunney

*For accompaniment see Leader's Guide, p.99*

© Copyright 1996 by ThreeFold Amen Music and Mother's Heart Music/ASCAP.
c/o ROM Administration, 8315 Twin Lakes Drive, Mobile, AL 36695. All Rights Reserved. Used by Permission.

CODA

We lift up the banner of faith, We lift up the banner of hope, We lift up the banner of pow'r over us.

Jesus is the banner, Jesus is the banner, Jesus is the banner, over us, over us, over us.

# Made for Praise

*Words and Music by*
**DICK and MELODIE TUNNEY**
*Arranged by Dick Tunney*

**Bright shuffle** (♩ = 132)

CHOIR *mf*

When God made the heav-ens and earth — Ev-'ry-thing had a plan, — The moon at night — and the sun — by day, — At on-ly His com-mand. — And when the Lord — made me, — He knew what I'd do best. — I was made — to praise — Him — with joy and thank-ful-ness! Like a bird was made to fly, — And the sun was made to shine. —

*For accompaniment see Leader's Guide, p.109*

© Copyright 1997 Sony/ATV Tunes LLC/Molto Bravo! Music, Inc./Dick & Mel Music (ASCAP). All rights administered by Sony/ATV Music Publishing, 8 Music Sq. W., Nashville, TN 37203. Used by permission.

God has a pur-pose for ev-'ry-one, __ For your life and for mine. __ He has been so good to me, __ My heart and voice I'll raise. __ For all __ of my days, I __ was made for praise. __ How can I __ keep si-lent? I'm gon-na make a joy-ful noise __ To tell the world __ what my God __ has done __ for ev-'ry girl and boy. __ 'Cause when the Lord __ made me __ He knew what I'd do best. __

I was made to praise Him with joy and thankfulness! Like a bird was made to fly, And the sun was made to shine. God has a purpose for ev-'ry-one, For your life and for mine. He has been so good to me, My heart and voice I'll raise. For all of my days, I was made, For all of my days, I was made, For all of my days, I was made for praise!

# Softly and Tenderly

Words and Music by
WILL L. THOMPSON
Arranged by Dick Tunney

Gently (♩ = 92)   CHOIR   *mp*

1. Soft-ly and ten-der-ly Je-sus is call-ing, Call-ing for you and for me;
2. Oh! for the won-der-ful love He has prom-ised, Prom-ised for you and for me;

See, on the por-tals, He's wait-ing and watch-ing, Watch-ing for you and for me.
Though we have sinned He has mer-cy and par-don, Par-don for you and for me.

(opt. div.)
Come home, come home, __ come home, __ You who are wea-ry come home; __ Ear-nest-ly, ten-der-ly,

*Third time to Coda*

Je-sus is call-ing, Call-ing, O sin-ner, __ come home!

*D.S. al Coda*

sin-ner, __ come home! __ Come

**CODA**

sin-ner, __ come __ home! __

*For accompaniment see Leader's Guide, p.163*

© Copyright 1998 Sony/ATV Tunes LLC/Molto Bravo! Music, Inc./Dick & Mel Music (ASCAP). All rights administered by Sony/ATV Music Publishing, 8 Music Sq. W., Nashville, TN 37203. Used by permission.

# CHORAL READING

ALL: All things were created by God!

SOLO 1: Like...

SOLO 2: Cats and bats,

SOLO 3: Fleas and bees,

SOLO 4: Bears and hares,

SOLO 5: And even monkeys.

SOLO 6: But amazing as all of these...

SOLO 7: God made Jesus...who died for me!

26

27

# WHALE OF A TALE

Feel the steady beat in "Whale of a Tale" by using your pointer finger to tap the beat. Listen to the recording and point to the pictures while feeling the steady pulse.

# Scripture Dynamics

Divide the students into three groups. Then follow these directions:
1. Teach each group their one or two measure repeated rhythmic phrase.
2. Have the different groups learn the dynamic patterns listed below.
   • Note: Practice separately.
3. After each group has mastered their rhythms and dynamics, perform the chants at the same time and listen to the lovely terraced dynamics that have been created.

*This activity can be done in one session or extended into several.*

| A. | 2x - Forte | B. | 2x - Rest | C. | 1x - Piano |
|---|---|---|---|---|---|
|    | 4x - Piano |    | 2x - Forte |    | 2x - Rest |
|    | 2x - Forte |    | 4x - Piano |    | 1x - Piano |

**A.** Seek first His king - dom.

**B.** They will be giv - en all of these.

**C.** All of these things will be giv - en to you if you seek His king - dom and righ-teous-ness first.

*f*
*mp*
*mf*
*p*
*f*
*mp*
*p*
*mf*

| | |
|---|---|
| 𝄌 | *D.S. al Coda* |
| ♭♭♭ | $\frac{4}{4}$ |
| 1. | 2. |
| ‖: | :‖ |

# Your Awesome Singing Machine

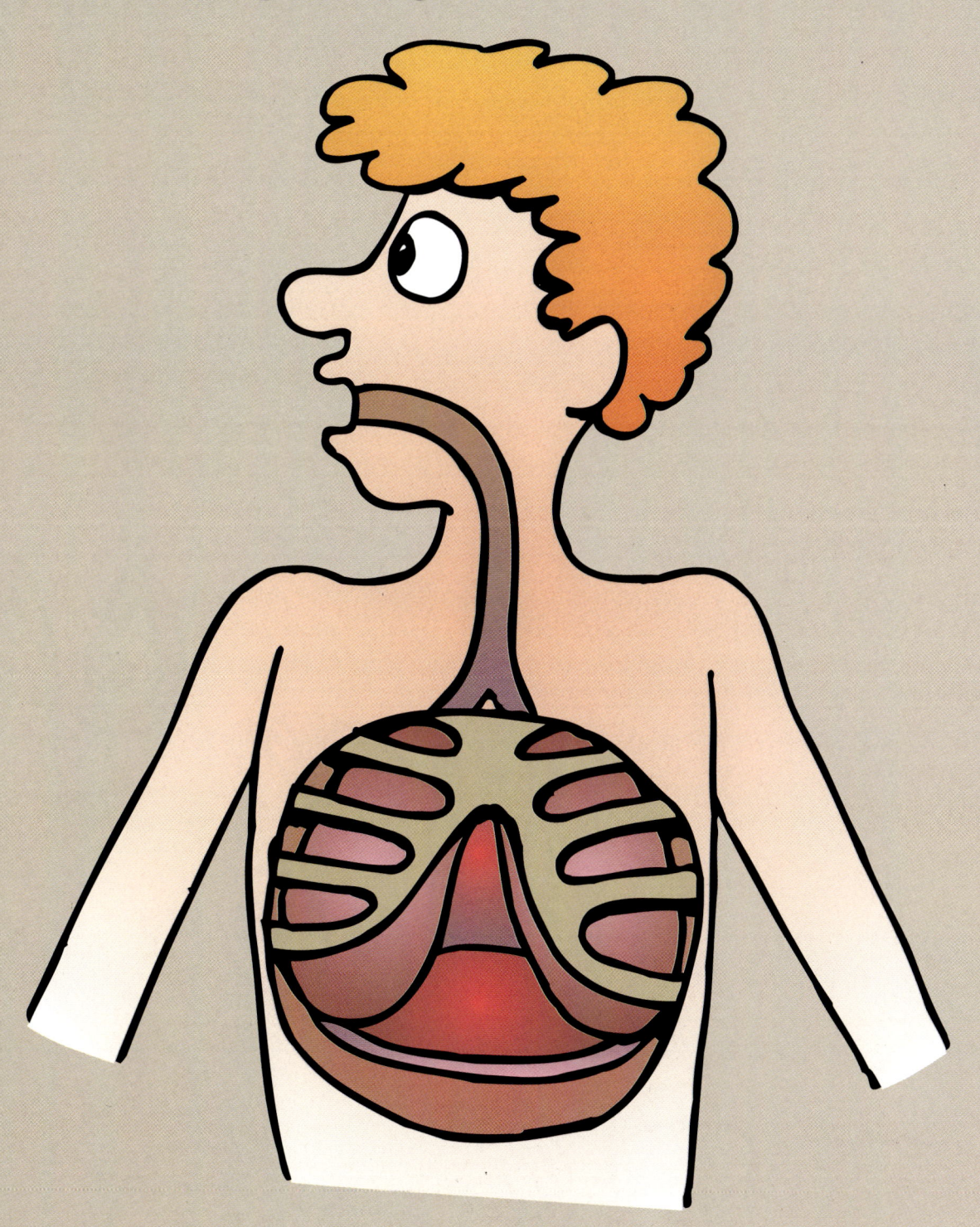

## WHALE OF A TALE *FINGER PLAY*

There was one man named Jonah. ................................*Hold up one finger*

God told him, "Go to the city of Ninevah and tell ..............*Walk with two fingers*
them to come back and worship Me."

The one man, Jonah, did not listen to God and ................*Hold up one finger*
went on a boat to the city of Tarshish.

Jonah went into the hull of the boat and went ..................*Sleep with hands folded together*
to sleep. *creating a pillow for your head.*

While Jonah was sleeping on the boat, ...........................*Take both index fingers and strike*
it began to rain. *them together creating the sound*
*of light rain.*

It began to rain harder. ......................................................*Use all fingers to make rain.*

Then the Lord hurled a great wind on the sea ..................*Slap thighs with hands*
and it rained even harder. *making rain.*

There was a great storm on the sea; it seemed ................*Make wind sounds with mouth;*
the boat Jonah was on would fall apart. *continue to slap thighs but add*
*stomping feet to create the storm*

The captain of the boat found Jonah and shook ..............*Use hands to shake Jonah.*
him to wake him up.

He said, "Get up, call your God. Perhaps your
God can save us."

Jonah got up and said, "I worship the God who ................*Use hands to*
made the sea and the land. I have disobeyed *show waves*
my God; He has caused this storm. Throw me *of sea.*
overboard; then the sea will become calm."

The men did not want to throw Jonah over
board, so they desperately rowed the boat to
get to land. ............................*Use hands to*
*row the boat.*

But the storm did not stop.  So, they threw ......................Use hands to throw Jonah.
Jonah overboard.

The sea stopped raging.  And a great fish ......................Use hands to form a fish;
swallowed Jonah.                                                                  eating Jonah.

Jonah was in the fish for three days and three nights. ....Hold up three fingers.

While Jonah was in the fish, he prayed to God. ..............Pray, with palms
And asked God to forgive his disobedience.                      touching palms.

God heard Jonah's prayer and the fish coughed
Jonah out on dry land.

Now, the Lord spoke to one man, Jonah, again.  ............Hold up one finger
God said, "Jonah go to the city of Ninevah and
tell them to come back and worship me."

This time Jonah walked to Ninevah and preached ..........Walk with two fingers
as God told Him to do.

The people of Ninevah heard Jonah and prayed ............Pray, with palms
to God and told God they were sorry for disobeying.      touching palms.

God heard their prayer and was glad.

**THE END!**

# Fire Drill

**Characters**:
Off Stage Voice
Sara
Cindy
Jennifer

**SCENE UP ON A GROUP OF THREE CHILDREN IN A LINE. THEY ARE EXITING A SCHOOL BUILDING WITH FRIGHTENED EXCITEMENT. AN ALARM IS RINGING.**

OFF STAGE VOICE: Please leave the building immediately. Stay in line, remain quiet and do as your teacher instructs.

SARA: How do you know if this is a fire drill or the real thing?

CINDY: Well, we don't. It's just that we have a drill once a month, so that we know what to do if we have a real fire.

JENNIFER: (EXCITEDLY) Didn't we just have a drill about a week ago?

CINDY: Noooo....maybe two weeks ago.

SARA: Oh no....then there really is a fire.

CINDY: We don't know that...calm down. They probably wanted to do the drill early because of the school calendar or something.

SARA: Oh my gosh...what's gonna happen? I left my puppy back pack in there. And what about all my books and papers?

**SFX OF SIRENS**

JENNIFER: Listen...here come the fire trucks.

SARA: See, there really is a fire.

CINDY: Cool it...you guys...they probably just sent a truck out to check out the building. It's nothing.

SARA: How do you know?

| | |
|---|---|
| CINDY: | Well...I don't know...(LOOKING) but I don't see any smoke or flames or anything. |
| JENNIFER: | How can you stay so calm? Aren't you scared? |
| CINDY: | Of course I'm scared....it's just.... |
| SARA: | Just what? |
| CINDY: | Well, it's funny but a Bible verse just keeps coming back to my mind.... "Do not fear for I am with you." |
| SARA: | What does that mean? |
| CINDY: | It means God knows all the good and bad things that will happen to us...but He will be with us while those things are happening. |

# INVESTIGATIVE REPORT

**Reporter:** This is Scoop Jackson with News from Mr. Noah. Mr. Noah... we have just received an unconfirmed report that you are building an ark because you think rain is coming.

**NOAH:** Yes, I am building an ark.

**Reporter:** It looks like you are expecting a large crowd on your ship...

**NOAH:** Yes...It's a big ark...it has three decks and is 300 cubits long and 30 cubits high and is 50 cubits wide.

**Reporter:** Four questions for you, Mr. Noah...why, when, how and who? First of all...why are you building an ark? We have been in a drought situation for at least 2 years now.

**NOAH:** I'm building an ark because God told me to.

**Reporter:** Who will be placed on the ark with you?

**NOAH:** My family and two of every animal on the earth.

**Reporter:** *(NOT BELIEVING)* So your family will be going with you on the ark. Again, how is this vessel going to float... you are not near any major seaport?

**NOAH:** It will float... because God said it would.

# – News About Noah

Reporter: And Mr. Noah...how will you get all the creatures of the earth on the ark?

NOAH: I will do it with my God's help.

Reporter: Are you telling me you will get two of every creature on earth on this ship you are building?

NOAH: That's correct...two of each bird, animal and every creeping thing will be on this ark.

Reporter: And when will you, shall we say, "Set Sail?"

NOAH: We will get in the ark when God tells us to and then I believe it will begin to rain.

Reporter: How long will you be in this ark?

NOAH: As long as God tells me to.

Reporter: Mr. Noah...don't you feel a little foolish building a ship with no water around or no water in sight?

NOAH: No, because I believe that God told me to do this and I believe He will send a flood. Would you like to come on the ark with us?

Reporter: No way, Mr. Noah. It's all a little too much for me to believe. This is Scoop Jackson reporting with Noah News.

# Add - A - Word

God

God gave

God gave Him

God gave Him the

God gave Him the name

God gave Him the name that

God gave Him the name that is

God gave Him the name that is above

God gave Him the name that is above every

God gave Him the name that is above every name

Philippians 2:9

# HEART JIVE

Clap the rhythm patterns below. Then perform each rhythm pattern making the suggested sound. Try the sound composition in a round

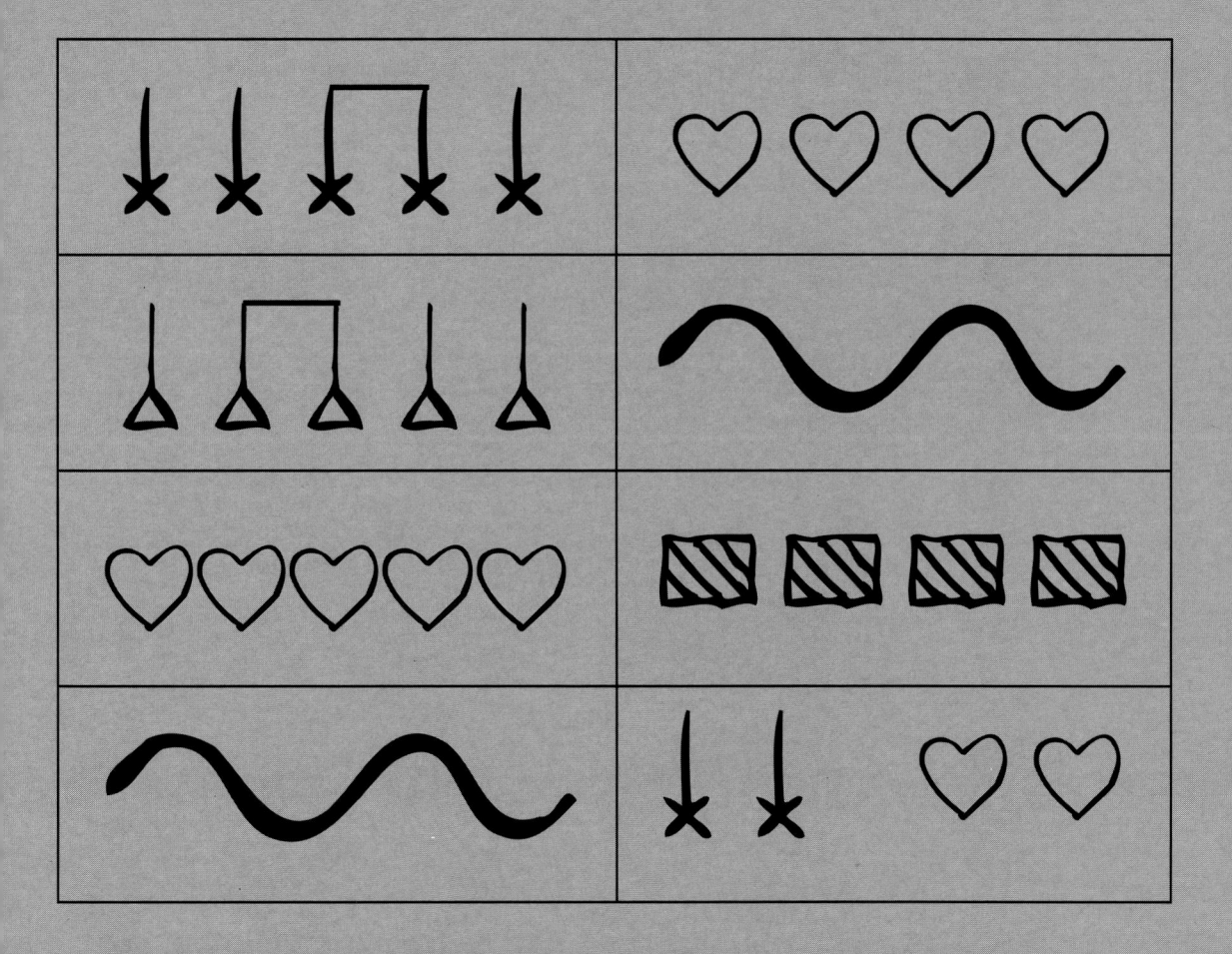

♡ — PAT HEART WITH RIGHT HAND

∿ — OO...

𝄻 — CLICK TONGUE

𝄻 — SMACK LIPS

▨ — BUZZ

# More than Anything

Words and Music by
JON MOHR and RANDALL DENNIS
Arranged by Dick Tunney

*With a Calypso feel* (♩ = 138)

CHOIR

God loves peo-ple more than an-y-thing. God loves peo-ple more than an-y-thing More than an-y-thing He wants them to know He'd rath-er die than let them go, 'Cause

*Third time to Coda*

God loves peo-ple more than an-y-thing

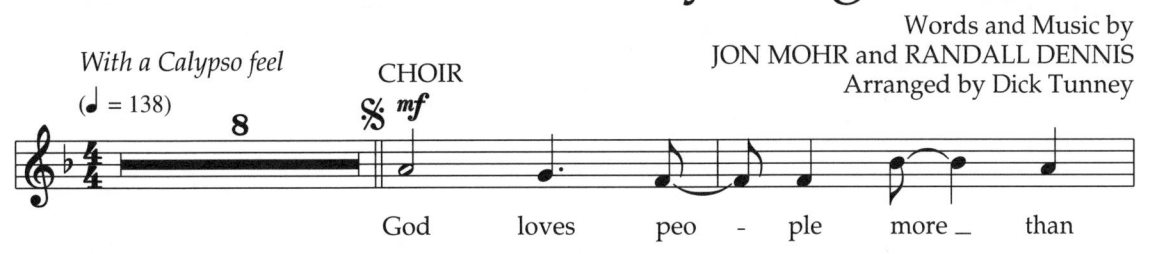

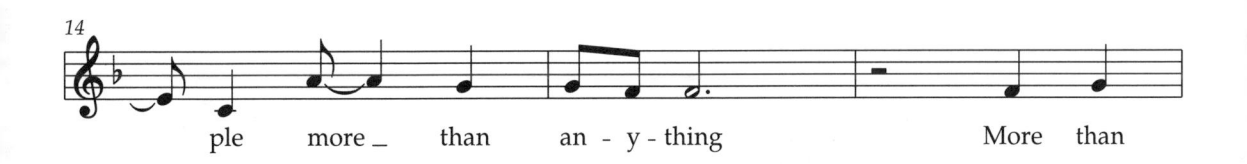

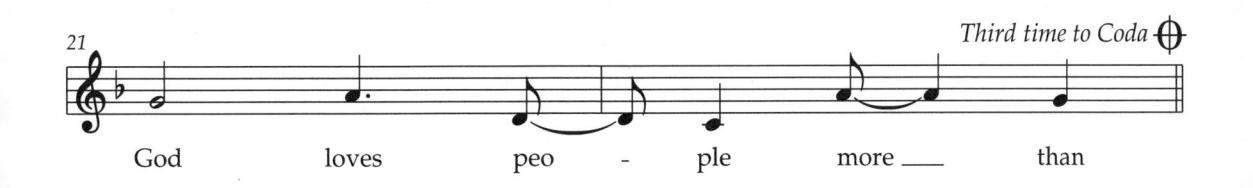

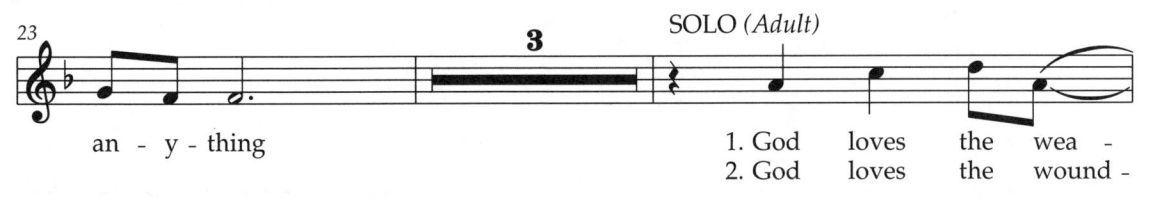

SOLO (Adult)

1. God loves the wea-
2. God loves the wound-

*For accompaniment see Leader's Guide, p.123*

© Copyright 1995 Sony/ATV Songs LLC d/b/a Tree Publishing Co./Randy Cox Music, Inc. (BMI)/Sony/ATV Tunes LLC d/b/a Cross Keys Publishing Co./Molto Bravo! Music, Inc. (ASCAP). All rights administered by Sony/ATV Music Publishing, 8 Music Sq. W., Nashville, TN 37203. Used by Permission.

ry when they're too weak to try;
ed who've stum-bled in-to sin.

He feels their pain, He knows
He reach-es down and pulls

their shame, He cries with those who cry.
them out And cleans them off a-gain.

He won't give up or walk
And He will heal the bro-

a-way when oth-er peo-ple
ken heart that's giv-en up on

do, 'Cause God loves peo-
love, 'Cause God loves peo-

*D.S. al Coda*

ple more than an-y-thing.
ple more than an-y-thing.

**CODA**

*rit.*

an-y-thing.

# Nobody But Noah

*Words and Music by*
TOM McBRYDE and JANET McMAHAN-WILSON
*Arranged by Dick Tunney*

Driving (♩ = 100)   CHOIR

No one knew the news ___ that No-ah knew, ___ no-bod-y but No-ah. No one knew e-nough to know ___ what No-ah knew to do. ___ No-bod-y but No-ah e-ven had a clue, ___ Why, or when, or how, or who.

*Third time to Coda*

No one knew the news ___ that No-ah knew. ___ No-bod-y but No-ah No-ah

SOLO 1 *(spoken)* No-ah knew ___ dry land was

SOLO 2 *(spoken)* 'bout to be-come mud.

SOLO 3 *(spoken)* No-ah knew ___ God planned to bring ___ a-bout a great ___ big flood.

SOLO 4 *(spoken)* No-ah knew ___ that

SOLO 5 *(spoken)* CHOIR *(sung)* when he got his ship ___ in shape He could

*For accompaniment see Leader's Guide, p.135*

© Copyright 1998 Van Ness Press, Inc. (ASCAP).
Distributed by GENEVOX (a div. of GMG), Nashville, TN 37234.

42

round up all the an-i-mals and make their great es-cape.

**CODA**

No-ah. No one knew the news that No-ah knew, nobod-y but No-ah. No one knew e-nough to know what No-ah knew to do. No-bod-y but No-ah e-ven had a clue. Why, or where, or how, or who. No one knew the news that No-ah knew. No-bod-y but No-ah e-ven had a clue, Why, or where, or how, or who. No one knew the news that No-ah knew. No-bod-y but No-ah!

# Psalm 91 Lullaby

Words and Music by
SCOTT BRASHER and MERRILL FARNSWORTH
Arranged by Dick Tunney

Gently (♩ = 84)

SOLO

Do not be a-fraid.

Do not be a-fraid. The One who made the heav-ens____ will guard your night and day.

Call up-on His name. Call up-on His
Do not be a-fraid. Do not be a-

name. And He will hear your cry, And
fraid. The

keep all harm a-way.

Oh, fear not sweet chil-dren for

*For accompaniment see Leader's Guide, p.143*

© Copyright 1997 Sony/ATV Tunes LLC/Molto Bravo! Music, Inc. (ASCAP). All rights administered by Sony/ATV Music Publishing, 8 Music Sq. W., Nashville, TN 37203. Used by Permission.

He is near. Take shelter now under His wings. Angels will guard you, nothing will harm you. His love will comfort you.

*D.S. al Coda*

**CODA**

One who made the heavens will guard you night and day. The One who made the heavens will guard you night and day.

# Seek First the Kingdom

Words and Music by
JOHN CHISUM and NANCY GORDON
Arranged by Dick Tunney

Steady (♩ = 104)

Seek first the king - dom, ___ seek first the king - dom of God. ___

Seek first the king - dom, ___ seek first the king - dom of God, ___

And His righ - teous - ness, ___

and His righ - teous - ness. ___ And

*Third time to Coda*

all ___ these things ___ shall be add - ed un - to you.

add - ed un - to you. ___

*For accompaniment see Leader's Guide, p.153*

© Copyright 1996 Word Music (a div. of WORD, INC.)/ThreeFold Amen Music, Inc. and
Mother's Heart Music (ASCAP) c/o ROM Administration, 8315 Twin Lakes Drive, Mobile, AL 36695.
All Rights Reserved. Used by Permission.

46

Don't wor-ry a-bout tomor-row. To-mor-row will wor-ry a-bout its own things. Suf-fi-cient for the day is its own trou-ble.

*D.S. al Coda*

**CODA**

add-ed un-to you. And His righ-teous-ness, and His righ-teous-ness. And all these things shall be add-ed un-to you.

*rit.*

# Sunday School Medley

*Brightly* (♩ = 138)     CHOIR *f*     Arranged by Dick Tunney

*I've got the joy, joy, joy, joy, down in my heart, down in my heart, down in my heart. I've got the joy, joy, joy, joy down in my heart, down in my heart to stay. And I'm so hap-py, so ver-y hap-py, I have the love of Je-sus in my heart, down in my heart. And I'm so hap-py, so ver-y hap-py. I have the love of Je-sus in my heart. I've got the joy, joy, joy, joy down in my heart, down in my heart, down in my heart. I've got the joy, joy, joy, joy down in my heart, down in my heart to stay.*    *Shuffle feel*    **If you're

*"I've Got the Joy," Words and music by GEORGE W. COOKE.
**"If You're Happy," Traditional.

*For accompaniment see Leader's Guide, p.171*

© Copyright 1998 Sony/ATV Tunes LLC/Molto Bravo! Music, Inc./Dick & Mel Music (ASCAP). All rights administered by Sony/ATV Music Publishing, 8 Music Sq. W., Nashville, TN 37203. Used by Permission.

hap - py and you know it clap your hands. *(hand claps)* If you're

hap - py and you know it clap your hands. If you're

hap - py and you know it then your face will sure - ly show it If you're

hap - py and you know it clap your hands. If you're

hap - py and you know it, High five! *(spoken)* If you're

hap - py and you know it, High five! *(spoken)* If you're

hap - py and you know it then your face will sure - ly show it. If you're

hap - py and you know it, High five! *(spoken)* If you're

*rit.* hap - py and you know it then your face will sure - ly show it. *(even eighths)*

*(shuffle)* *a tempo* If you're hap - py and you know it, *High* *(spoken)*

five! *Al - le - lu, al - le - lu, al - le - lu, al - le - lu - ia, Praise ye ___ the Lord! Al - le - lu, al - le - lu, al - le - lu, al - le - lu - ia, Praise ye ___ the Lord!

**GROUP 1**
Praise ye ___ the

**GROUP 2** Lord! Al - le - lu - ia! **GROUP 1** Praise ye ___ the

**GROUP 2** Lord! Al - le - lu - ia! **GROUP 1** Praise ye ___ the

*Faster* (♩ = 132)
**GROUP 2** Lord! Al - le - lu - ia! **GROUP 1** Praise ye! **ALL** **Praise ___ Him, praise ___ Him, praise Him in the morn - ing, praise Him at the noon - time. Praise ___ Him, praise ___ Him, praise Him when the sun goes down. Love ___ Him,

*"Allelu, Alleluia," Traditional.
**"Jesus in the Morining," Traditional.

love \_\_\_\_ Him, love Him in the morn - ing,

love Him at the noon - time. Love \_\_\_\_ Him,

love \_\_\_\_ Him, love Him when the sun goes down.

*rit.*

Love Him when the sun goes down.

*Spoken:* Jesus said, "Let the little children come to me, and do not hinder them. For the kingdom of heaven belongs to such as these."

*Slowly* (♩ = 84)

*Je - sus loves the lit - tle

chil - dren, all the chil-dren of the world. Red and

yel - low, black and white, they are pre - cious in His sight. Je - sus

SOLO **Yes, Je - sus loves me,

loves the lit - tle chil-dren of the world.

Yes, Je - sus loves me, Yes, Je - sus

loves me, \_\_\_\_ The Bi - ble tells me so. The

*"Jesus Loves the Little Children," Words by C. H. WOOLSTON. Music by GEORGE F. ROOT.
**"Jesus Loves Me," Words by ANNA B. WARNER. Music by WILLIAM B. BRADBURY.

*"Do, Lord," Traditional.

# Tell Him Thank You

Words and Music by
NANCY GORDON
Arranged by Dick Tunney

*Brightly* ($\quarternote = 88$)

Ev-'ry morn-ing tell Him, "Thank You, thank You."
Ev-'ry eve-ning tell Him, "Thank You, thank You."
Ev-'ry morn-ing tell Him, "Thank You, Lord."
Ev-'ry eve-ning tell Him, "Thank You, Lord."
Ev-'ry noon-time tell Him, "Thank You, thank You."
All the time I'll tell Him, "Thank You, thank You."
Ev-'ry noon-time tell Him, "Thank You, Lord."
All the time I'll tell Him, "Thank You, Lord."

Thank You, thank You, thank You, Lord. Thank You, thank You, thank You, Lord. Thank You, thank You, thank You, Lord. Thank You, thank You, thank You, Lord. Thank You, Lord. Thank You, Lord.

*For accompaniment see Leader's Guide, p.187*

© Copyright 1996 by ThreeFold Amen Music and Mother's Heart Music (ASCAP).
c/o ROM Administration, 8315 Twin Lakes Drive, Mobile, AL 36695.
All Rights Reserved. Used by Permission.

# There Is Power in the Wonderful Name

Words and Music by
ARNOLD MANKE
Arranged by Dick Tunney

*Funky* ($\quarternote$ = 138)

CHOIR *mp*

1. There is
(2. There is)

pow - er in the name of Je - sus! There is
glo - ry in the name of Je - sus! There is

pow - er in the name of Je - sus! There is
glo - ry in the name of Je - sus! There is

pow - er in the name of Je - sus! There is
glo - ry in the name of Je - sus! There is

pow - er in that won - der - ful name.
glo - ry in that won - der - ful name.

2. There is

*mf*

There is heal - ing in the

name of Je - sus! There is heal - ing in the

*For accompaniment see Leader's Guide, p.197*

© Copyright 1984 New Spring Publishing, Inc./ASCAP, a div. of Brentwood-Benson Music Publishing, Inc.
All Rights Reserved. Unauthorized duplication prohibited.

54

name of Jesus! There is healing in the name of Jesus! There is healing in that wonderful name. There's salvation in the name of Jesus! There's salvation in the name of Jesus! There's salvation in the name of Jesus! There's salvation in that wonderful name. There is glory in that wonderful name. There is power in that wonderful name! Oh, yeah!

# Whale of a Tale

Words and Music by
LOWELL ALEXANDER
Arranged by Dick Tunney

Rhythmic (♩ = 152)

SOLO *mf*

Lord, I know in my heart Should have done what You wished. Now I'm praying here in the dark in the belly of this fish.

1. Lord, I will not hide, I'll try to never fear. And how can I say no to You, after all that's happened here. It seems like a whale of a tale But

2. Lord, I will not fail You, I will go and I will preach. If only You'll deliver me down the tongue and past those teeth.

*For accompaniment see Leader's Guide, p.209*

© Copyright 1996 Sony/ATV Songs LLC/Randy Cox Music, Inc. (BMI). All rights adminstered by Sony/ATV Music Publishing, 8 Music Sq. W., Nashville, TN 37203. Used by Permission.

it's the on - ly truth.

God may have to rock the boat If we

won't do what He wants us to.

It's hard to stom - ach; I'm in a

fish be - neath the blue. Seems like a

*Third time to Coda*

whale of a tale But

I'm God's liv - ing proof.

*D.S. al Coda*

I'm God's liv - ing proof. It seems like a

**CODA**

I'm God's liv - ing proof. It seems like a whale of a tale

But I'm God's liv - ing proof.

# With My Whole Heart

Words and Music by
BILLY CROCKETT and KENNY WOOD
Arranged by Dick Tunney

Simply (♩ = 112)

CHOIR *mf*

1. With my whole heart,
(2. With my) whole mind,

Lord, let me love You with my whole heart,
Lord, let me love You with my whole mind,

none a-bove You, praise and love You
none a-bove You, praise and love You

with my whole heart. With my
with my whole mind. With my

whole heart, Lord, let me hear You with my
whole mind, Lord, let me hear You with my

whole heart ev-er near You;
whole mind ev-er near You;

Help me hear You with my whole heart.
Help me hear You with my whole

2. With my mind.

*For accompaniment see Leader's Guide, p.219*

© Copyright 1983 New Spring Publishing, Inc./ASCAP, a div. of Brentwood-Benson Music Publishing, Inc.
All Rights Reserved. Unauthorized duplication prohibited.

3. With my whole life, Lord, let me love You with my whole life, none above You; praise and love You with my whole life. With my whole life, Lord let me hear You with my whole life, ever near You; help me hear You with my whole life. Help me hear You with my whole life.

# You Are Always in His Sight

Words and Music by
JANET McMAHAN-WILSON
Arranged by Dick Tunney

*Gently* (♩ = 92)

*For accompaniment see Leader's Guide, p.229*

To order *Made for Praise*®,
contact your l,ocal music supplier
or call the Customer Service Center

TOLL FREE at 1-800-458-2772

FAX: 615-251-5933

E-Mail: CustomerService@bssb.com

Customer Service Center,
MSN 113
127 Ninth Avenue North
Nashville, TN  37234